This book belongs to

• •

First published 2011 by Brown Watson
The Old Mill, 76 Fleckney Road,
Kibworth Beauchamp, Leic LE8 0HG

ISBN: 978-0-7097-1918-2

My First

ABC

a

a is for apple

b

b is for butterfly

C

C is for car

d is for dinosaur

e

e is for elephant

f is for frog

g

g is for gorilla

h

h is for helicopter

i

i is for ice cream

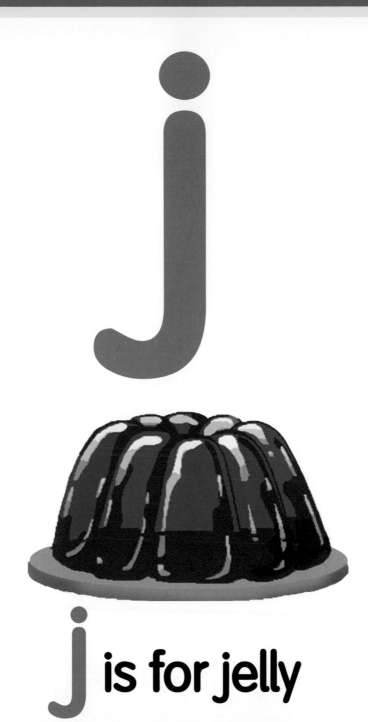

j is for jelly

k

k is for kangaroo

l is for lamb

m

m is for monkey

n

1 2 3

n is for numbers

O

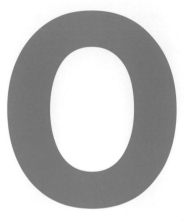

O is for octopus

p

p is for pencil

q

q is for queen

r

r is for rabbit

S

s is for strawberry

t

t is for teddy

U

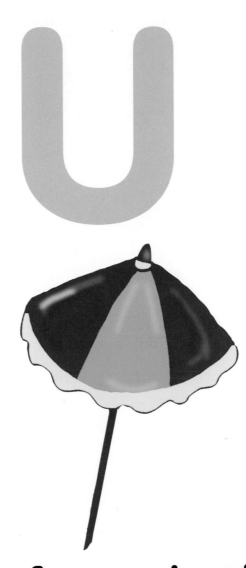

U is for umbrella

V

V is for violin

W is for whale

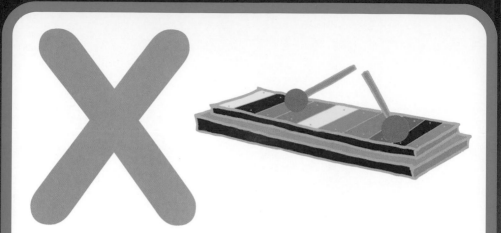

x is for xylophone

y is for yacht

Z

Z is for zebra